Marigold

Textbook in English for Class I

राष्ट्रीय शैक्षिक अनुसंधान और प्रशिक्षण परिषद्
NATIONAL COUNCIL OF EDUCATIONAL RESEARCH AND TRAINING

ISBN 81-7450-478-8

First Edition
February 2006 Phalguna 1927

Reprinted
November 2006 Kartika 1928
October 2007 Kartika 1929
January 2009 Magha 1930
November 2009 Kartika 1931
November 2010 Kartika 1932
January 2012 Magha 1933
December 2012 Agrahayana 1934
October 2013 Asvina 1935
November 2014 Agrahayana 1936
May 2016 Vaishakha 1938
December 2016 Pausa 1938
November 2017 Agrahayana 1939

PD 325T RK

© *National Council of Educational Research*

₹ 55.00

OFFICES OF THE PUBLICATION DIVISION, NCERT

NCERT Campus
Sri Aurobindo Marg
New Delhi 110 016   Phone : 011-26562708

108, 100 Feet Road
Hosdakere Halli Extension
Banashankari III Stage
Bangaluru 560 085   Phone : 080-26725740

Navjivan Trust Building
P.O.Navjivan
Ahmedabad 380 014   Phone : 079-27541446

CWC Campus
Opp. Dhankal Bus Stop
Panihati
Kolkata 700 114   Phone : 033-25530454

CWC Complex
Maligaon
Guwahati 781 021   Phone : 0361-2674869

Printed on 80 GSM paper with NCERT watermark

Published at the Publication Division by the Secretary. National Council or Educational Research and Training. Sri Aurobindo Marg, New Delhi 110 016 and printed at Berry Art Press, A-9, Mayapuri Industrial Area, Phase-I, New Delhi-110 064

Publication Team

Head, Publication Division : *M. Siraj Anwar*

Chief Editor : *Shveta Uppal*

Chief Business Manager : *Gautam Ganguly*

Chief Production Officer (In-charge) : *Arun Chitkara*

Production Assistant : *Sunil Kumar*

Cover, layout and Illustrations

Henu Mehtani

Foreword

The National Curriculum Framework, 2005, recommends that children's life at school must be linked to their life outside the school. This principle marks a departure from the legacy of bookish learning which continues to shape our system and causes a gap between the school, home and community. The syllabi and textbooks developed on the basis of NCF signify an attempt to implement this basic idea. They also attempt to discourage rote learning and the maintenance of sharp boundaries between different subject areas. We hope these measures will take us significantly further in the direction of a child-centred system of education outlined in the National Policy on Education (1986).

The success of this effort depends on the steps that school principals and teachers will take to encourage children to reflect on their own learning and to pursue imaginative activities and questions. We must recognise that given space, time and freedom, children generate new knowledge by engaging with the information passed on to them by adults. Treating the prescribed textbook as the sole basis of examination is one of the key reasons why other resources and sites of learning are ignored. Inculcating creativity and initiative is possible if we perceive and treat children as participants in learning, not as receivers of a fixed body of knowledge.

These aims imply considerable change in school routines and mode of functioning. Flexibility in the daily time-table is as necessary as rigour in implementing the annual calendar so that the required number of teaching days are actually devoted to teaching. The methods used for teaching and evaluation will also determine how effective this textbook proves for making children's life at school a happy experience, rather than a source of stress or boredom. Syllabus designers have tried to address the problem of curricular burden by restructuring and reorienting knowledge at different stages with greater consideration for child psychology and the time available for teaching. The textbook attempts to enhance this endeavour by giving higher priority and space to opportunities for contemplation and wondering, discussion in small groups, and activities requiring hands-on experience.

NCERT appreciates the hard work done by the textbook development committee responsible for this book. We wish to thank the Chairperson of the advisory group at primary level, Professor Anita Rampal and the Chief Advisor for this book, Professor R. Lalitha Eapen (CIEFL, Hyderabad) for guiding the work of this committee. Several teachers contributed to the development of this textbook; we are grateful to their principals for making this possible. We are indebted to the institutions and organisations which have generously permitted us to draw upon their resources, material and personnel. We are especially grateful to the members of the National Monitoring Committee, appointed by the Department of Secondary and Higher Education, Ministry of Human Resource Development under the Chairpersonship of Professor Mrinal Miri and Professor G.P. Deshpande, for their valuable time and contribution. As an organisation committed to the systemic reform and continuous improvement in the quality of its products, NCERT welcomes comments and suggestions which will enable us to undertake further revision and refinement.

Director
National Council of Educational
Research and Training

20 December 2005
New Delhi

Textbook Development Committee

CHAIRPERSON, ADVISORY COMMITTEE FOR TEXTBOOKS AT THE PRIMARY LEVEL

Anita Rampal, *Professor*, Central Institute of Education, Delhi University

CHIEF ADVISOR

R. Lalitha Eapen, *Professor*, English and Foreign Languages University (EFLU), Hyderabad.

CHIEF COORDINATOR

Ram Janma Sharma, Former *Professor* and *Head*, Department of Education in Languages, NCERT, New Delhi.

MEMBERS

Anju Khanna, *Principal*, The Circle, New Delhi.

Meenu Kumar, *PGT*, Rajkiya Pratibha Vikas Vidyalaya, Vasant Kunj, Delhi.

Nita Berry, *Children's Literature Specialist*, New Delhi.

Rekha Johnson, *Primary Teacher*, Demonstration School, RIE, Ajmer.

Shobha Chanana, *TGT*, Kendriya Vidyalaya, Sagar, Madhya Pradesh.

MEMBER-COORDINATOR

Usha Dutta, Former *Professor*, Department of Education in Languages, NCERT, New Delhi.

Acknowledgements

National Council of Educational Research and Training is most grateful to the following for their valuable contributions in the development of this book – R. Amritavalli, *Professor,* CIEFL, Hyderabad, M.L. Tickoo, *Professor (Retd.),* CIEFL, Hyderabad and Sonika Kaushik, *Primary Teacher,* Sanskriti School, New Delhi.

The Council also thanks the following authors, copyright holders for permission to use poems and stories included in this book.

After a Bath by Aileen Fisher; *The Bubble, the Straw and the Shoe* by Alexei Tolstoy from Russian Tales for Children, E.P. Dutton and Company Inc., New York; *One Little Kitten* by Carolyn Graham; *Lalu and Peelu* by Vineeta Krishna, Ratnasagar, 1994; *Mother Hen and the Chicks*, The Beacon Readers 'At Old Lobs' by E.H. Grassam, Ginn and Company Ltd., London, 1951; *Mittu and the Yellow Mango* by Chitra Narendran, Frank Educational Aids Pvt. Ltd., New Delhi; *Merry-Go-Round* by Dorothy W. Baruch; *Circle* by Manorama Jafa, Ratnasagar Pvt. Ltd.; *Our Tree* by Pranab and Smita Chakravarti, National Book Trust, India, 2005; *Sundari* adapted from 'Cleo' by Ruth Dixon in 'The Children's Treasury,' compiled by Marjorie Barrows, Consolidated Book Publishers, Chicago, 1947; *The Tiger and the Mosquito* by Mrinalini Srivastava, translated by Alaka Shankar, Children's Book Trust, New Delhi, 2003 and *Anandi's Rainbow* by Anup Ray, National Book Trust, India, 2004. We also acknowledge Bharat Gyan Vigyan Samithi *Picture Stories* by Nikolai Radlov, New Delhi 2004 for *Giant Rat* and *Umbrella Nest*; Central Institute of English and Foreign Languages (CIEFL), Hyderabad for *Beginning Reading Programme, 2000* and C*ome on Everybody, Let's Sing* by Lois Birken Shaw Fleming.

Special thanks are due to Shveta Uppal, *Chief Editor,* NCERT and Vandana R. Singh, C*onsultant Editor* for going through the manuscript and suggesting relevant changes.

The Council also gratefully acknowledges the contributions of Rituraj Sharma, *DTP Operator;* Keerti Lingwal, *Proof Reader;* Sunanda, *Copy Editor* and *Incharge Computer Station,* Parash Ram Kaushik in shaping this book. Last but not the least, the efforts of the Publication Department, NCERT are highly appreciated.

CONTENTS

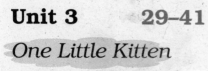

THE CONSTITUTION OF INDIA

PREAMBLE

WE, THE PEOPLE OF INDIA, having solemnly resolved to constitute India into a [1][SOVEREIGN SOCIALIST SECULAR DEMOCRATIC REPUBLIC] and to secure to all its citizens :

JUSTICE, social, economic and political;

LIBERTY of thought, expression, belief, faith and worship;

EQUALITY of status and of opportunity; and to promote among them all

FRATERNITY assuring the dignity of the individual and the [2][unity and integrity of the Nation];

IN OUR CONSTITUENT ASSEMBLY this twenty-sixth day of November, 1949 do **HEREBY ADOPT, ENACT AND GIVE TO OURSELVES THIS CONSTITUTION.**

---

1. Subs. by the Constitution (Forty-second Amendment) Act, 1976, Sec.2, for "Sovereign Democratic Republic" (w.e.f. 3.1.1977)
2. Subs. by the Constitution (Forty-second Amendment) Act, 1976, Sec.2, for "Unity of the Nation" (w.e.f. 3.1.1977)

A Happy Child

Enjoy this poem

My house is red - a little house;
A happy child am I.
I laugh and play the whole day long,
I hardly ever cry.

I have a tree, a green, green tree,
To shade me from the sun;
And under it I often sit,
When all my play is done.

New words

cry   day   red   sun

Let's read

The sun shines in the sky.
I have a red pen.

Read and match the words with the pictures. Draw a line.

I am a boy.

I am a girl.

boy

girl

Fun with colours

Fill in the box with the right colour.

▶ What is the colour of the happy child's house?

▶ What is the colour of your house?

▶ What is the colour of the tree?

▶ What is the colour of the sun?

Let's talk

Is there a tree growing near your house?

▶ Tell us about the tree. Is it big or small?
▶ Do you like the tree? What is the name
  of the tree?

2

Let's share

There are many kinds of houses. Circle the ones you have seen.

hut

igloo

flat

bungalow

Let's draw

Draw your house here and talk about it.

How do you feel — ☺ ☹

▸ When you get a new dress?

▸ When you get hurt?

▸ When you share your things?

▸ When you are ill?

Draw and say

 happy

 sad

⋯ _____

⋯ _____

Draw lines from the house to the people who live in your home.

My grandfather

My grandmother

My father

My home

My mother

My brother

My sister

Trace the numbers on the dotted lines.

1	2	3	4	5	6
one	two	three	four	five	six

How many people live in your house?

Write here. _____ people live in my house.

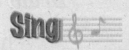

Jack-in-the box
Sits so still,
Won't you come out?
Yes, I will!

4

Join the dotted lines.

Write

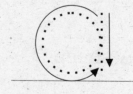

Look in a mirror. What do you see?
Draw your face in this circle.

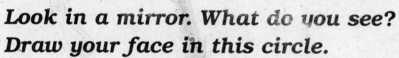

Read: a, b, c.
Write: a a a a a

5

Collect pictures of a cat, a cow, a dog and a sheep from old books or newspapers and paste them below.

A cat

A cow

A dog

A sheep

Trace over the dotted lines and complete the monkey's tail.

Monkey, monkey on a tree,
Swing, swing, swing, swing.

The following have lost their babies. Trace along the maze using different colours and find them. One has been done for you.

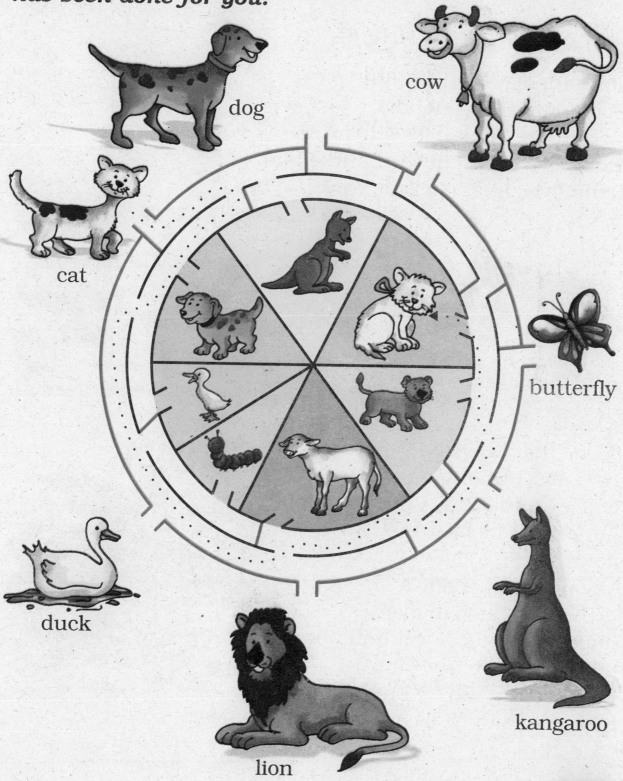

dog

cow

cat

butterfly

duck

lion

kangaroo

Three Little Pigs

Once there were three little pigs,
Sonu, Monu and Gonu.
    Sonu lived in a house of straw.
Monu lived in a house of sticks and
Gonu lived in a house of bricks.

    One day a big bad wolf came to Sonu's house.
He said, "I will huff and puff and I will blow your
house down." So he huffed and he
puffed and he blew the house
down.
    Sonu ran to Monu's house.
The wolf came to Monu's
house. He said, "I will huff and
puff and I will blow your
house down." So he huffed and
he puffed and he blew Monu's house down.

Sonu and Monu ran to Gonu's house.

The wolf came to Gonu's house. He said, "I will huff and puff and I will blow your house down." So he huffed and he puffed but he could not blow the brick house down. It was very strong.

The wolf went away and Sonu, Monu and Gonu lived happily together in the red brick house.

New words

and   bad   big   but   not   one   pig   the   was

Let's read

The wolf was big and bad.
The pig was not big.

9

Reading is fun

▸ How many pigs were there?
▸ What did the big wolf say to the pigs?

Let's talk

▸ Was the wolf good or bad?
▸ What is your house made of?

Let's share

▸ Who is good?
▸ Who is bad?

pig

wolf

Let's act

▸ Imagine you are at home when the wolf huffs and puffs.
▸ Act out the story of the wolf and three pigs.

Say aloud

1. One   4. Four

2. Two   5. Five

3. Three   6. Six

Let's draw

Join the dots from 1 to 10 to make the house. Then colour the picture.

There are farm animals, water animals and jungle animals in this picture. Help the animals reach their homes. Draw lines.

hen

dog

horse

crocodile

bear

frog

buffalo

FARM

12

cow

monkey

giraffe

rhinoceros

JUNGLE

WATER

Sing

'Bow wow', says the dog,
'Mew mew', says the cat,
'Bleat bleat', says the goat,
'Roar roar', says the lion,
'Hello, hello', says the child.

The emphasis in this book is on developing language skills by using the mother tongue in the initial stages. The teacher's encouragement and motivation are very important. Children are curious and love to try things in their own little ways. Do not correct their mistakes. Focus on the process of learning and remember that the child needs to be given activities that are exciting and stimulating.

The **first Unit** is about introducing the child to a process of learning following the concept *'from near to far'*. Allow them to talk and help them to express their thoughts by use of their mother tongue, visuals, pictures, sketches, single word questions and answers. As you introduce the text (both the poem and the story), encourage all the children to participate.

▸ **Develop listening skills**

Read the poem/story aloud to the children.

Read it with emphasis on clear speech and correct pauses at commas and full stops.

▸ **Develop pronunciation**

Let the children read aloud after you. Make them repeat

> *blow, flow, glow*   *brick, kick, stick*   *huff, puff, stuff*

▸ **Exposure to language**

Use *sight words* in the classroom by putting visuals and cue cards. Let children read these:

bad	*bed*	*big*	*cot*	*bun*
sad	*red*	*dig*	*hot*	*sun*

▸ **Develop speaking skills**

1. Encourage children to walk and jump like different animals. Let them make the sounds of *'huff'*, *'puff'* etc. with force.
2. Write two-letter words on the blackboard such as ***am***, ***he***, ***in***, ***is***, ***it***, ***me***, ***my***, ***so*** and start a contextual conversation by saying, *'She is a girl'*, *'I am a teacher'*, *'Please give me a pencil'*, *'He is a boy'*, *'You are so far away'*, *'It is a warm/cold day'* etc.

Provide opportunities to children for working and playing together in small groups. It will promote interaction, togetherness and team spirit besides encouragement for natural expressions.

3. Conversation based on 'Role play'
   - Divide your class into four groups: **Red**, **Yellow**, **Blue**, **Green**
   - Let each group make a house.

     Red— *a hut*　**Blue**— *a flat*　**Yellow**— *a bungalow*　**Green**— *an igloo*

     Red and **Blue** groups have to talk about all the objects in their houses.

     Yellow and **Green** groups have to talk about objects around their houses.

     - **Method**— Each group uses low-cost waste material (e.g. newspapers, cardboard, grass, leaves, matchsticks, etc.) to draw, sketch, construct or act out a scene from their house.

> **MATERIAL REQUIRED**
> ———◆———
>
> Boxes/old cartons for collecting leaves, twigs...
>
> Pencils / spoons, beads, string etc.

▶ **Develop writing skills / fine motor coordination**

Writing needs practice before it becomes spontaneous and neat. In making the strokes show the child how to hold the pencil and use it safely. Encourage children to make different patterns/basic strokes by drawing them on the blackboard, slate/paper. Put two letter and three letter words on flash cards and show them to the children. Let them recognise the words.

▶ **Raising awareness**

Talk about turning off taps and not wasting water.

After a Bath

Enjoy this poem

After my bath
I try, try, try
to wipe myself
till I'm dry, dry, dry.

Hands to wipe
and fingers and toes
and two wet legs
and a shiny nose.

Just think how much
less time I'd take
if I were a dog
and could shake, shake, shake.

Aileen Fisher

New words

dog   how   met   try   two

Let's read

I try to save water.
I have two ears, two legs, ten toes and one nose.

16

Let's talk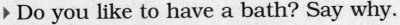

▸ Do you like to have a bath? Say why.
▸ Can you bathe yourself?
▸ How do you dry yourself?
▸ Have you seen an animal drying itself?

Let's share

Put a ⬭ around what you do after a bath.

Throw the wet towel on the floor.

Hang the wet towel to dry.

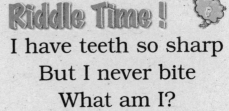

Riddle Time !
I have teeth so sharp
But I never bite
What am I?
Ans.: A comb

Do you wear these things?
Draw lines from the picture
to the word.

a. shirt **b.** socks **c.** cap **d.** trousers **e.** belt **f.** shoes

Let's do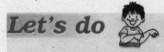

Match the following to make pairs. One has been done for you.

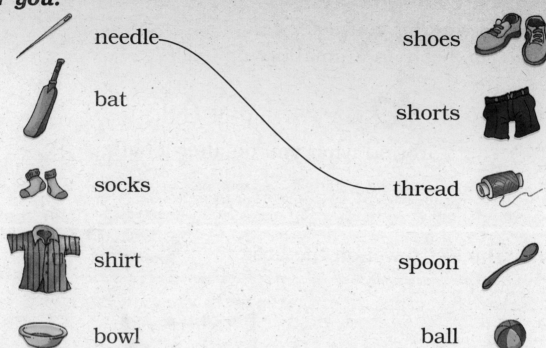

needle — shoes

bat — shorts

socks — thread

shirt — spoon

bowl — ball

Let's draw

Draw or stick a picture of yourself and your friend here. Then complete the sentences and say them aloud.

My name is

_____

My friend's name is

_____

Me   My friend

Trace the path to the flowers.

19

e e e   f f f

Trace over the waves and colour the fish.

u u u   v v v   w w w

b c d e f

The Bubble, the Straw and the Shoe

Once upon a time there lived a Bubble, a Straw and a Shoe.

One day they went into the forest.

They came to a river. They did not know how to cross it.

The Shoe said, "Bubble, let us float on you."

21

"No, Shoe! Let Straw stretch himself from one bank to the other. Then we can cross the river."

So, the Straw stretched himself from one bank to the other.

When the Shoe jumped on the Straw, it broke. The Shoe fell into the water with a loud splash.

The Bubble shook and shook with laughter and burst with a big bang.

Alexei Tolstoy

New words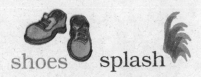

bank   bubble   burst   cross   river   shoes 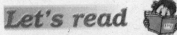 splash

Let's read

I can blow bubbles.
I can wear shoes.

22

Reading is fun

- ▸ Name the three friends.
- ▸ Where did they go one day?
- ▸ What did they want to do?

Let's talk

- ▸ How do you make bubbles?
- ▸ What do you wear on your feet?
- ▸ How would you cross a river?

Let's share

Put these doing words into the sentences.

jumped	shook	stretched	burst

The Straw _____ himself from one bank to the other.

The Shoe _____ on the Straw.

The Bubble _____ and _____ with laughter

and _____ with a big bang.

Let's draw

Trace the journey of a tadpole.

puddle   pond   lake   river

Draw the bubbles. Trace and say the letters aloud.

Sing

Hop a little, jump a little
One two three.
Run a little, skip a little
Tap one knee.
Bend a little, stretch a little
Nod your head.
Yawn a little, sleep a little
In your bed.

24

Match the balls with their numbers. Now trace the numbers.

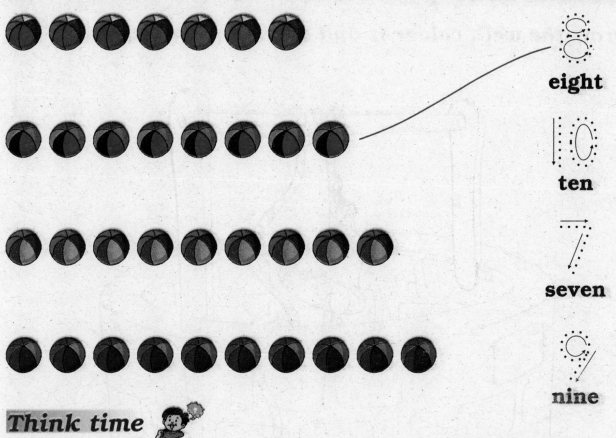

eight

ten

seven

nine

Think time

Look at these objects. Put them into a tub of water. Say which one will float and which one will sink.

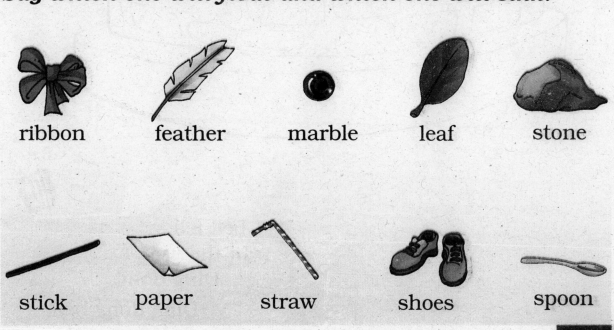

ribbon   feather   marble   leaf   stone

stick   paper   straw   shoes   spoon

Learn to write

Draw the well, colour it and say the rhyme aloud.

Sing

A bell fell
In the well.
Ding dong,
Ding dong bell.

Conversation is a very important and natural activity for the development of vocabulary and speech patterns. In Unit 2, involve all the children in these joyful interactive sessions. Encourage them with phrases such as, "Please try", or "Oh! You are so good!" Appreciate every child's efforts and ensure a feeling of success for all the children. Consider the abilities of each child.

▶ **Develop listening skills**

Practise the poem and say it aloud to the children.

Read the story with emphasis on new words and enable them to bring experiences into reading for understanding and enriching their imagination.

▶ **Develop pronunciation**

Read the text and say aloud with the children

cry, dry, try   dog, fog, log   dine, fine, mine   cake, shake, take

▶ **Exposure to language**

Use *sight words* in the classroom by putting visuals and cue cards. Let the child read these:

draw	hen	pit	dog	blue
straw	pen	wit	log	glue

▶ **Develop speaking skills**

1. Have a talk on brushing teeth, washing hands, hygiene etc.
2. Conversation based on 'Role play'
   - Divide the class into four groups Red, Yellow, Blue, Green

   Group Red: Let them say, 'I try to save water' as they wipe themselves with towels.

   Group Blue: Involve the children in an activity e.g. cleaning the cobwebs with sticks/mops or tidying the classroom or class cupboard. Let them say, 'I try to clean my space.'

   Group Yellow: Mix some soap in a bowl of water. Stir it to build up bubbles. Use it for the floating/sinking activity if you like.

   Group Green: Let them pick up papers, wrappers etc. from the school playground and put them into dustbins.
   - All groups are to make cutouts which can be hung in the class/outdoors/on the door/on the walls/on the trees.

- Imagine you are walking down a street and you see a friend far away. Wave out and call your friend.

▸ **Develop writing skills / fine motor coordination**

1. (a) Write on the blackboard *a, e, i, o, u* and **1 to 10**. Let the child write numbers and trace a few letters. These are the child's attempts at writing. The teacher can gradually lead the child to proper formation of letters. Also provide each child with a comfortable writing position, adequate space and an appreciative atmosphere.

   (b) Each child's grip on the pencil and appropriate colouring within lines must be looked into.

   (c) Use Activity Sheets to further encourage the patterns as on pages 19, 20, 23, 24, 25 and 26 and numbers 1 to 10 (here co-ordinate with the maths teacher). However, do not force the child.

2. Enact a situation when your writing hand is hurt and you have to write.

3. Show children how to open and close buttons/zip and tie shoelaces.

▸ **Raising awareness**

Talk to the children about switching off lights, fans etc. when not required.

MATERIAL REQUIRED
◆
Any old clothes with buttons, purse / bag with a zip, shoes with laces.

One Little Kitten

Listen and enjoy this poem

One little kitten
Two big cats
Three baby butterflies
Four big rats
Five fat fishes
Six sad seals
Seven silly seagulls
Eight happy eels;
Nine nervous lizards
Ten brave bees
Eleven smelly elephants
Twelve fat fleas
Thirteen alligators
Fourteen whales
Fifteen donkeys
With fifteen tails.

Carolyn Graham

New words

cat   fat    rat   sad   ten

Let's read

A fat cat saw a rat

Reading is fun

▸ How many kinds of creatures are there in the poem?
▸ Are the seals happy?

Let's talk

▸ Where do the fish live?
▸ What are the other things found in water?
▸ There are many creatures in the poem. Which ones have you seen?
▸ Tell us about when you feel —

sad   **brave**

happy   **nervous**

Let's share

Make faces to show your feelings to your friends.

sad

brave

nervous

happy

Let's draw

Look at the pictures of the animals given below and underline them in the poem. Then trace the letters.

kitten

butterfly

cat

rat

fish

seal

seagull

eel

lizard

bee

elephant

flea

alligator

whale

donkey

am	he	if	in	is
it	me	my	no	of
on	so	to	us	we
all	and	bad	big	bit
but	can	cat	cry	day
dog	fat	let	met	not
one	pig	ran	red	sad
saw	sit	sun	ten	the
try	two	was	wet	you

Look and read

Say these words aloud. Then match them with the pictures by drawing lines.

bag   tin   hen   pen   tap   axe   ant   fox   cap   cot

Fill in the blanks from the words given above.

b _ g   h _ n   t _ p   c _ p   t _ n

c _ t   _ nt   p _ n   f _ x   _ xe

33

Lalu and Peelu

Listen and enjoy this story

There was a hen.
She had two chicks,
Lalu and Peelu.
  Lalu was red.
He loved red things.
  Peelu was yellow.
He loved yellow things.
  One day Lalu saw
something on a plant.
It was red. He ate it up.
  Oh, no! It was a red chilli.
It was very hot.
  Lalu's mouth started
burning.
He screamed.

Mother Hen came running.
Peelu came too.
Peelu said, "I'll get something for you!"
Peelu brought a yellow laddu.

Lalu gobbled up the laddu.
His mouth stopped burning.
Mother Hen and Lalu kissed Peelu.

Vineeta Krishna

New words

chicks   hen   hot   plant   yellow

Let's read

I love plants.
The chicks ran to their mother.

Reading is fun

▸ Name the chicks in the story.
▸ Who liked yellow things?
▸ What did Lalu eat one day?

Let's talk

▸ Peelu brought a yellow laddu for Lalu. What are the other things Peelu could have brought that are both yellow and sweet? Name at least two, e.g. a mango.

Let's share

▸ Lalu loves red things. Peelu loves yellow things. The colour red is called 'lal' in Hindi and yellow is called 'peela'. What do you call these colours in your language?

▸ Give names to these chicks using the names of some other colours in your language.

Lalu _____

Peelu _____

_____

_____

Let's write

Match the chicks to the eggs they have hatched from.
One has been done for you.
Trace the letters on the eggs *a e i o u* .

Let's draw

Trace and colour these flowers.

Yellow sunflower

Bluebells

Riddle Time !

Red plus yellow is orange
Red plus blue is purple
Blue plus yellow is green
Add white to make them light.

Red rose

Mother Hen and the Chicks

Let's act

Come to me, chicks.
I want you here.

What do you
want, mother?

Look at me.
Do what I do.
Down and up.
Up and down.

Mother! Mother!
I can do what you do.
Look at me.
Down and up.
Up and down.

Act out this story with the class.

Adapted from E.H. Grassam

39

While working with the children provide them with activities that are interesting and challenging. Give opportunities for fun to the children and encourage early writing attempts. Help them to develop the skill to identify and discriminate objects, pictures, colours, shapes etc.

▶ **Develop listening skills**

Recite the poem to the children using appropriate actions/gestures.

Read the story with emphasis on new words and make sentences with reference to the story.

▶ **Develop pronunciation**

Read the text and say aloud with the children

ate, date, gate	*boy, joy, toy*	*burn, turn*	*bees, fleas*

▶ **Exposure to language**

Use *sight words* in the classroom such as visuals and cue cards. Let the children read these:

a	*e*	*i*	*o*	*u*

▶ **Develop speaking skills**

The little play on chicks can introduce vocabulary in an interesting, conversational way.

1. Have a talk on eating healthy food.
2. Conversation based on 'Role play'
   ● Divide the class into four groups Red , Yellow , Blue , Green

   Group Red: to make paper bags.

   Group Blue: to collect leaves for eyes, nose, ears.

   Group Yellow: to roll a string/play dough for whiskers.

   Group Green: to roll a rope/twigs to make tails.

All groups will join to complete the paper bags. The children can decorate them with animal faces or figures. Afterwards these can be used as hand puppets. You can encourage the children as they go about doing this activity. Add any other material that you may want.

> **MATERIAL REQUIRED**
> ───◆───
>
> Any old paper bags/ newspapers, glue, thread, rope, coloured pencils and markers.

- Imagine you are eating a fruit and it falls down. Ask the children what they would do.
- Act out a situation when (i) you are hungry (ii) you are full (iii) you overeat.

▸ Develop writing skills / fine motor coordination

1. Write the words *hat*, *bed*, *pin*, *hot*, *cut* and numbers **11** to **20** on the blackboard. Let the child write numbers and read from the board. Use Activity Sheets to further encourage the patterns as on pages 31, 33 and 37 and numbers 11 to 20 (here co-ordinate with the maths teacher). However, do not force the child.

2. Sorting things into groups is an essential part of learning. By differentiating between objects, children start to think about similarities and differences and how things can be categorised. Show children how to sort leaves and twigs by placing them in two different piles.

3. Give children coloured beads and ask them to string them in a sequence. For example, one blue bead, two red beads and so on. Or on a string, thread two or three beads and ask the children the number of beads.

▸ Raising awareness

Tell the children to wash their hands before and after meals.

Once I saw a Little Bird

Sing and enjoy this poem

Once I saw a little bird
Come hop, hop, hop,
I cried, "Little bird,
Will you stop, stop, stop?"

I was going to the window
To say, "How do you do?"
But he shook his little tail
And away he flew.

New words

bird   hop   stop   tail   window

Let's read

The bird flies out of the window.
We must stop cutting trees.

42

Reading is fun

▸ What did the child see?
▸ What was the little bird doing?

Let's talk

▸ Do you see any birds around your school or your house?
▸ Have you tried talking to them?

Let's do

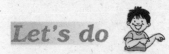

Join the letters from a to z.

43

Trace over the dotted lines and letters. Now colour the stars.

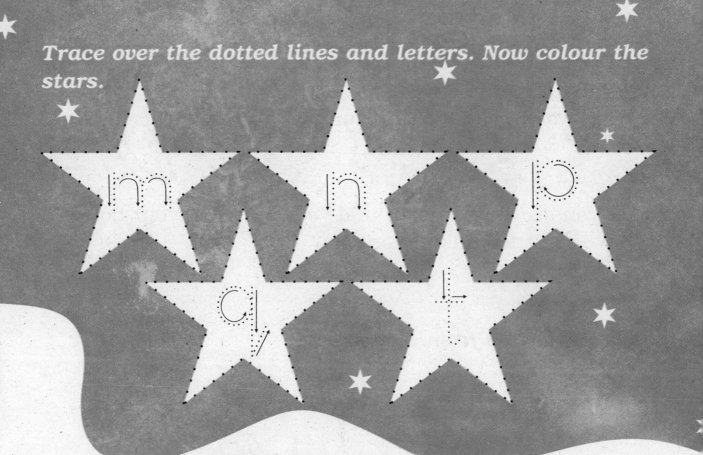

Say these words aloud and talk about the picture. Then tick the right colour.

| roof | door | windows | walls | floor | plants | dustbin |

The roof is **pink / blue**.

The walls are **yellow / red**.

The windows are **green / brown**.

The door is **blue / grey**.

The dustbin is **pink / green**.

The plants are **green / orange**.

The floor is **grey / brown**.

Mittu and the Yellow Mango

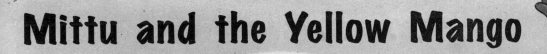

Listen and enjoy this story

Mittu was a parrot.
A green parrot
with a red beak.
   One day Mittu
was flying.
He loved to fly.
He looked down.
He saw a big yellow
mango on a tree.

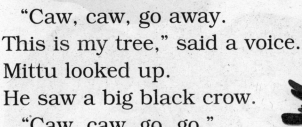

Mittu liked mangoes.
"I want to eat that yellow mango,"
he said.
He flew down to the tree.

   "Caw, caw, go away.
This is my tree," said a voice.
Mittu looked up.
He saw a big black crow.
   "Caw, caw, go, go,"
the crow shouted.
He had a very loud voice.
Mittu was afraid of the crow.
He flew away.

45

Mittu saw a red balloon.
It was under a tree.
He had an idea.
  He picked up the red balloon.
He was careful not to burst it.
  He flew to the mango tree.
The crow was sitting on the tree.
Mittu went behind the tree.

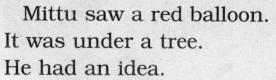

  He pecked the balloon with his red beak.
"Pop!" The balloon burst.
It made a loud noise.

  "Caw!" said the crow.
And he fell off the tree.
"Caw, caw, a big gun is after me," said the crow.
  He flew away.
He never came back to the tree.

Mittu came to the tree.
He ate the big yellow mango.
   "Yummy yummy,
what a nice mango!" he said.
He was very happy.
Clever Mittu!

Chitra Narendran

New words

black   crow    mango   parrot

Let's read

I like eating a mango.
I like feeding a crow.

Reading is fun

▸ What did Mittu see on the tree?
▸ What did the big black crow say?
▸ What did Mittu see under the tree?

Let's talk

▸ Do you like eating mangoes?
▸ Do you like green mangoes? Why?
▸ Do you like yellow mangoes? Why?

Let's share

Colour the chilli red and the parrot in colours of your choice.

Sing

Parrot with a red beak,
Can you really speak?
Mittu, Mittu,
Mittu, Mittu!

Trace the path of the lady bird.

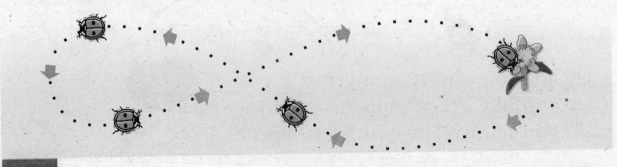

Match the fruit and vegetables to the trees they grow on.

banana

coconut

apple

grapes

mango

coconut
tree

apple
tree

banana
tree

mango
tree

grapevine

Learn to write

Draw over the dotted lines.

Say aloud

bat	bed	bit	dot	bun
cat	fed	hit	hot	fun
mat	red	pit	pot	run

Choose a letter from the box and complete the words below.

a	e	i	o	u

s_t   p_g   b_g   d_t   s_n

f_n   l_g   s_t   l_t   b_n

The children look forward to this active approach of hearing, doing and participating. Now they can be given the freedom to choose their groups and tasks. Groups can be divided into those who want to (i) taste something tangy like a lemon, (ii) sweet like sugar, (iii) bitter like neem/bitter gourd or (iv) salt. Let them make *nimbu pani* with the required ingredients and drink it. Shared activities will foster healthy relationships.

> **MATERIAL REQUIRED**
> ◆
>
> 2 lemons, a little sugar, a little salt, neem leaves and drinking water.

▸ **Develop reading skills**

By this time children should be able to read a few words. Involve them in a reading activity, laying emphasis on the highlighted words in the text.

▸ **Develop pronunciation**

Say aloud with the children

'Stop' says the red light,

'Go' says the green.

'Wait' says the yellow light,

Blinking in between.

▸ **Exposure to language**

Display *sight words* in the classroom. Sight word vocabulary is developed by using words repeatedly in meaningful contexts. Let children read these:

chilli   *mango*   *parrot*

▸ **Develop speaking skills**

1. The peacock is our national bird. The male bird has a beautiful tail. The female is called a peahen. Encourage children to talk about other birds they see in their school or near their homes.

2. Conversation based on 'Role play'

   ● At this stage children should be able to identify different sounds in their environment. Ask them to imagine that they are birds and let them call out to another bird. Encourage them to listen to sounds of nature (chirping of birds, rainfall, wind blowing etc.)

- Act out a scene when the children are birds flying in the sky.
- The children may be taken out and given their food outdoors. Let them be motivated to talk about different tastes after the meal or have a conversation about *nimbu pani* if the activity has been done.

▶ **Develop writing skills / fine motor coordination**

1. Write the following words and numbers on the blackboard — ***hop***, ***stop***, ***shop***, ***mop*** and digits from **1** to **10**. Use Activity Sheets and you can also start using a notebook to further encourage the patterns as on pages 43, 44, 48, 49 and 50.

2. Show the children how to draw a bird/ make a bird with clay/play dough.

▶ **Raising awareness**

Tell the class that birds are our friends. We can feed them with some grains or bread crumbs.

Merry-Go-Round

Listen, sing and dance

I climbed up on the merry-go-round,
And it went round and round.

I climbed up on a big brown horse,
And it went up and down.

Around and round
And up and down,
Around and round
And up and down.

I sat high up
On a big brown horse
And rode around
On the merry-go-round
And rode around

On the merry-go-round
I rode around

On the merry-go-round
Around
And round
And
Round...

Dorothy W. Baruch

New words

around   down   in   on   out   round   up

Let's read

I ride on a horse.

53

Reading is fun

▸ How did the merry-go-round go?
▸ How did the big brown horse go?

Let's talk

▸ Have you seen a merry-go-round?
▸ Where have you seen it?
▸ Would you like to go to a fair?

Let's share

▸ Look at this picture and describe the fair.
▸ Talk about the things you enjoy at a fair.

Go round the merry-go-round, circle the letters and say them aloud.

Circle

One day Mohini was sitting with her grandmother.
  Grandmother drew a circle.
"Can you draw a circle, Mohini?"
  "Yes I can."
  Soon Mohini drew a circle.

  "Now, I'll draw a ball."
Grandmother drew three lines on the circle.
  Mohini drew three lines on her circle.
It really looked like a ball.
  "Now let's draw a balloon."
Grandmother added a zig-zag line to the circle.

"Oh! It really looks like a balloon." Mohini clapped with joy.

Mohini drew many circles— big and small circles, red, blue, green and yellow circles. She also added zig-zag lines to these.

And now there were many balloons.

"Can you draw something else with a circle?" asked Grandmother.

"Yes," said Mohini.

She drew a wheel, a moon, a sun, a rabbit and her own face.

Manorama Jafa

New words

ball   blue   circle   lines   moon

Let's read

I can draw a circle.
The moon is round.

57

Reading is fun

▸ What did Grandmother and Mohini draw first?
▸ What were the colours of the balloons that Mohini drew?

Let's draw

▸ In the circles below draw—

what Grandmother drew   **what Mohini drew**

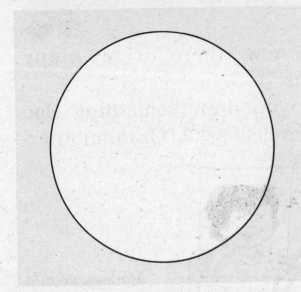 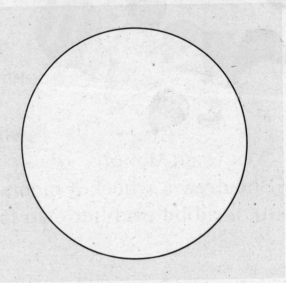

▸ Look at these shapes.

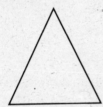  

Try making these shapes into
● a car
● a house
● a door
● anything else

58

**Draw along the dots. So, what did you make?
Can you make sounds like a train?**

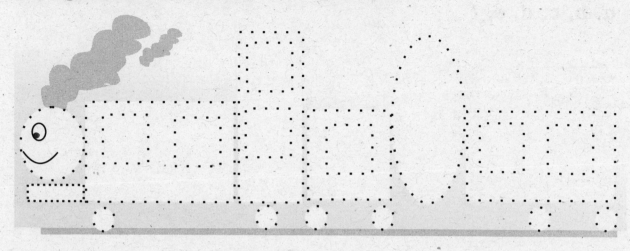

**Draw a face on the balloon below. One has been
done for you.**

a, b, c, d, e, f

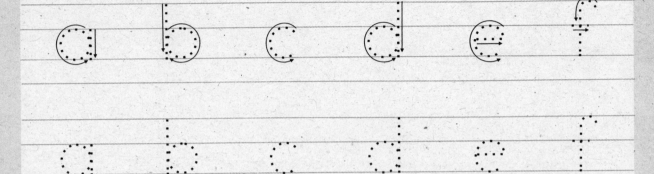

g, h, i, j, k, l

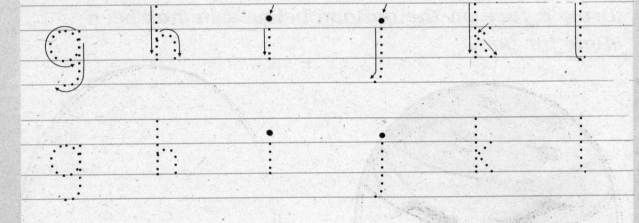

m, n, o, p, q, r

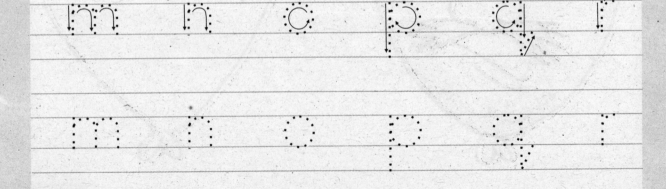

mango  nut orange peach

mango .... nut

orange .... peach

Look at the picture and fill in the blanks.

dog   d __ __

b __ __ __   bull

e __ __ __ __ __ __ __ __

elephant

owl   o __ __

h __ __ __ __

horse

cat   c __ __

Activities now have more to do with what the children like to do. You can try this:

- Make the children sit in a circle. Ask a child to start counting from number 1. The child sitting next to him/her continues with number 2 and so on. The child who has to say number 5 or 10 says *chup* and the next child starts with number 1 again.
- Draw a circle on the floor with a piece of chalk. Let the children walk along the drawn line. Ask them to hold a book/any object in one hand and walk along the line. Talk to them about balancing things. Ask them if they feel giddy on a merry-go-round.

▸ **Develop listening skills**

The children can be taken outdoors during the break and allowed to eat their snacks there. Let them talk to each other about the different tastes of foods. Ask children to speak to the point and take turns. Also inculcate in them a habit of listening when others speak.

▸ **Develop pronunciation**

Read the following words and say aloud with the children:

around   *bound*   *brown*   *down*

found   *ground*   *sound*

▸ **Exposure to language**

Display the following *sight words* in the classroom and let the children read them aloud.

| *circle* | *line* | *oval* | *square* | *triangle* | *zig-zag* |

▸ **Develop speaking skills**

Children can play 'Farmer's in the Den' or any other song of their choice.

The farmer's in the den,	*The farmer wants a wife,*
The farmer's in the den,	*The wife wants a child,*
Heigho-the cheerio,	*The child wants a nurse,*
The farmer's in the den.	*The nurse wants a dog,*
	The dog wants a bone.

▶ **Develop writing skills / fine motor coordination**

1. Write the letters from **a** to **q** on the blackboard. Let the children read and write from the blackboard and the picture dictionary. Children should not be forced or pressurised to recognise words or letters. This can be done through pictures or actions. Use Activity Sheets and a notebook to further encourage the patterns as on pages 55, 58, 59, 60 and 61, and any extra exercises that the children want to do.

2. Pour water from one container to another.

▶ **Raising awareness**

Tell the class that we must cover our food from flies.

MATERIAL REQUIRED
◆
2 glasses / cups / pots and water

If I Were an Apple

Learn, recite and enjoy this poem

If I were an apple
And grew on a tree,
I think I'd drop down
On a nice boy like me.
I wouldn't stay there
Giving nobody joy,
I'd fall down at once
And say, "Eat me, my boy!"

New words

apple   boy   eat   drop   joy

Let's read

I like to eat an apple.
We clap our hands with joy.

64

Reading is fun

 ▸ Where is the apple?
 ▸ Where is the boy?
 ▸ How can the boy get the apple?

Let's talk

 ▸ Do you like apples?
 ▸ Have you ever climbed a fruit tree?

Let's share

Fill in the blanks.

If I were a bird, I would_____. (fly, cry)

If I were a bee, I would_____. (buzz, chirp)

Let's read and write

s   t   u   v

Say aloud

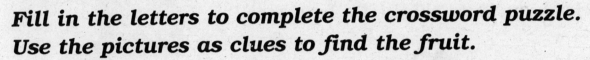

apple	drew	dew	ball
people	grew	few	call
ripple	threw	mew	fall

Word fun

Fill in the letters to complete the crossword puzzle. Use the pictures as clues to find the fruit.

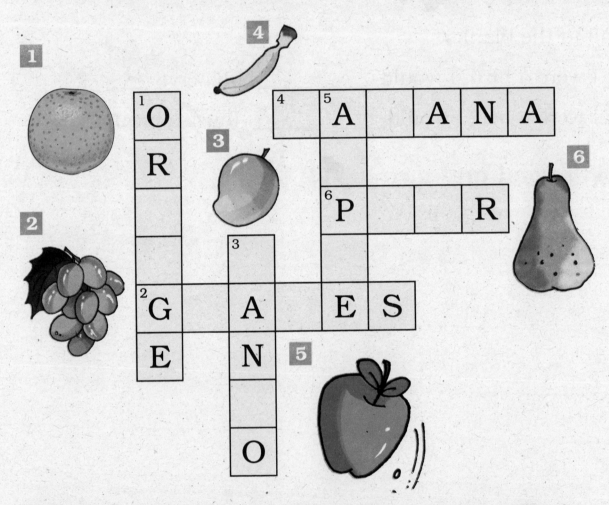

Which is your favourite fruit? Say why you like it, first in your own language and then in English.

Our Tree

A little bird sees
Ripe fruit on our tree
And eats a tasty berry.
The bird flies tall
And a berry seed falls.

The rains have come
Hurry! let's run.
Clouds, rain and sun...
Our plant is born, a little one.

Now a tree,
With branches long,
Crows and bird-song,
Crawling ants and spiders' webs,
Caterpillars with tiny legs,
Rich green leaves, life aplenty.

The tree has fruit,
Some big, some small,
Let us pluck them
But do not fall!

Crows perch, squirrels run,
And see the monkeys
Having fun!

Strong branches,
With pretty swings,
Our beautiful tree
Has so many things.

Pranab and Smita Chakravarti

New words

berry   caterpillars   nest   rain    tree

Let's read

Clouds bring rain.
The tree has branches.

Reading is fun

▸ Where does the little bird see the fruit?
▸ What does she do?
▸ What happens when she eats the berry?

Let's talk

▸ Where do birds live?
▸ Have you seen any birds near your house?
▸ Do you know their names in English or in your own language?

Let's share

Circle the things you can find on a tree.

beehive

clothes

kite

crows

pencil

leaves

ant

book

Juicy fruits

▶ Name the fruits you can see on the push cart.
Say which ones you like the most.

apples

pineapples

mangoes

bananas

grapes

oranges

I like <u>apples</u> the most.

Let's do

How does a seed grow? Look at the pictures below and
number them in the correct order.

I dig the earth.

I plant the seed.

I water the plant.

The plant grows.

Let's think

Put a tick (✓) if it is true. Put a cross (X) if it is not true.

	True	Not true
I like fruit.		
I like flowers.		
There is a tree near my house.		
The tree has flowers.		
The tree has fruit.		

Let's read and write

w x y z

71

Help the bird reach its nest.

▶ **Can you climb a tree?**
Yes, I can climb.
Yes, I can pluck.
Yes, I can catch.
Yes, I can jump.

Murali's Mango Tree

Listen, read and enjoy this story

One day Murali ate a mango.
He threw the seed behind his house.
Many months later, he saw a plant.
He watered the plant every day.
The plant grew into a big mango tree.

Every summer, many mangoes grow on it.
Now, Murali's children eat the mangoes.

Read the sentences and tick (✓) the right picture.

Murali ate a (banana  /mango) one day.

He threw the (seed /mango) behind his house.

Many months later, he saw a (seed /plant).

He watered the (seed /plant) every day.

Many (apples /mangoes) grew on the tree.

Draw a tree showing leaves, branches, fruit, birds, nest and a swing.

Let's talk

▸ Describe the picture using all the words given above.
▸ Should trees be cut?
▸ Name some trees which you have seen.

This unit is a good opportunity for involving children in interesting activities about their environment. Encourage children to look and listen attentively and express their thoughts freely.

- Talk to them about trees around and how important they are.

- Share with them topics like "Why do you think trees are important for us?"

Give them clues like, "They give us shade, flowers, fruits etc."

▶ **Group Activity**

Let the children make a class tree with their handprints. Let them stick leaves and twigs on it. Write this verse and stick it under a tree.

MATERIAL REQUIRED
◆
A sheet of paper, some twigs, some leaves and an old cardboard sheet

What do I plant?

When I plant a tree

I plant a circle of shade around me;

A circle of shade

Where people come

To rest under the sun.

▶ **Develop pronunciation**

Words like **tree, bee, flea** can be introduced.

▶ **Exposure to language**

This time let the *sight words* be the names of children which can be pasted on the tree that the children have made.

Names of all the children such as *Ritu*   *Kabir*   *Mohan*   *Lofang*

▶ **Develop speaking skills**

Give children a week or two to learn a rhyme, one in their language and one in English. Let them recite these. Always appreciate their efforts. Do not push children who are not ready for it. As facilitators we must let children speak at their own pace.

▸ Develop writing skills

Write the letters from **r** to **z** on the blackboard. Let the children read from the board and the picture dictionary. Encourage these early writing attempts and ensure a feeling of success for all children. Use Activity Sheets and a notebook to further encourage the patterns as on pages 65, 66, 69, 70, 71, 72 and 74.

▸ Use the method of developing fine motor coordination

Tell the class how to sort out three mixed pulses into different piles or sort leaves on the basis of their colour, shape and texture.

▸ Awareness raising

Have a discussion on the hazards of throwing things into the river and why we must stop this from happening.

A Kite

Learn and enjoy this poem

I often sit and wish that I
Could be a kite up in the sky,
And ride upon the breeze and go
Whichever way I chanced to blow.

New words

blow   breeze   chanced   kite   sit

Let's read

I can fly a kite.
I love to sit under a tree.

Reading is fun

▸ What does the child wish to be?
▸ What does the child wish to do with the breeze?

Let's talk

▸ What would you like to be?
▸ Imagine you are a bird in the sky. Describe what you will feel when you see a kite flying near you.

Say aloud

bride	cart
kite	chance
ride	dance
side	fast
sky	part

Do you know more words with these sounds?

Let's share

▸ What are the different things that fly in the sky?
▸ If you had wings, where would you fly?

Trace on the rain patterns.

Use the picture clues to draw pictures of the day sky and night sky in the windows.
Colour the pictures.

You see them all in the sky. Fill in the blanks by choosing words from the box.

stars	sun	cloud	rainbow	moon

_____

_____

_____

Sundari

Read and enjoy this story

Sundari was a big red, white and blue kite. When Bobby made her she smiled at him.

"You are beautiful and I will call you Sundari," he said.

One day, Bobby took Sundari to the fair.

The band was playing and everyone was smiling.

A merry-go-round was playing a happy little tune. It was carrying lots of boys and girls round and round on its wooden animals.

Bobby looked for an open space where he could run and fly his kite. Sundari looked too.

Out in the grass ran Bobby, holding up his kite as high as he could.

Puff! The wind came along. Sundari started to fly up! But she could not go very high. A little dog was holding on to her long tail. It was in his mouth.

80

Bobby shooed the dog away.

"We'll try again," Bobby said.

This time Sundari leaped up in the air. She tugged hard. Oh, how she wanted Bobby to let go of her string! She gave a big tug. Bobby had to let her go.

"Wheee!" cried Sundari. "Now I can fly as high as I please!"

And away she went. She flew up, up, up in the air.

(Adapted from 'Cleo' by Ruth Dixon)

New words

band   dizzy   smile   string   tug   wind

Let's read

I feel dizzy on a merry-go-round.
The band was playing a tune.

Reading is fun

- Who made Sundari?
- Why did Bobby call his kite 'Sundari'?
- Did Sundari fly very high at first?
- What made Sundari really happy?

Let's talk

- Do you like to fly kites?
- Who helps you to fly kites?

Let's share

- Tick the objects you need to fly a kite.
  Colour the kite.

stick   roller   glue   pair of scissors

basket   paper   ball

Name the objects in your own language.

82

Trace over the dotted lines

Let's do

Look at the pictures and tell the story in your own words.

THE UMBRELLA AND THE CROW

Rearrange the following sentences in the right order to make it into a story on the left page.

▶ A wind blows.
▶ It is raining.
▶ The crow flies away with the umbrella.
▶ The girl has an umbrella.
▶ The umbrella is now a nest.
▶ The umbrella hangs from a tree.

Now say the story in English using the words rain, wind, crow, nest, is, has, blows, flies.

Let's read and write

crow   girl   nest

crow   girl   nest

tree   wind

tree   wind

In this unit we introduce children to sounds like *blow, whoosh, puff, whiff, dizzy, shooed, shoo, woof,* and *woo*. Encourage children to listen to all the sounds on their way to school. Let them discuss the ones that were pleasant and those that were not. You can also ask them to recite different rhymes involving animal sounds.

▶ **Develop pronunciation**

Have a reading session of the story 'Sundari'. Let each child be given a few lines to read.

▶ **Exposure to language**

Continue to use *sight words* in the classroom. Here you can put up the following words and get the children to repeat after you.

door   **tree**   **window**

▶ **Develop speaking skills**

Divide your class into four groups: **1** , **2** , **3** , **4**
Enjoy this short play with children saying:

All children	:	1, 2, 3, 4, 5
Group-1	:	*Whoosh! Whoosh!* Once I caught a fish alive.
Group-2	:	6, 7, 8, 9, 10
		Woof! Woof! Then I let it go again.
Group-3	:	11, 12, 13, 14, 15
		Shoo! Shoo! Why did you let it go?
Group-4	:	16, 17, 18, 19, 20
		Blow! Blow! Because it bit my finger so.
Group-1, 2, 3	:	Which finger did it bite?
Group-4	:	This little finger on my right.

Let all children clap their hands and say this entire rhyme once again.

Through play, children develop the habit of establishing and following instructions which will help them throughout their lives. Playing in groups helps them to exercise self control. It also gives an opportunity to the teacher to observe and improve children's social understanding and attitudes.

▸ Develop writing skills / fine motor coordination

Introduce *A* to *Z* in capital letters. Write from *a* to *z* on the blackboard. Let the children write and read from the board and from the picture dictionary. Use Activity Sheets and a notebook for further practice.

Let children move in a single line saying, "*Puff, puff* goes the train".

▸ Raising awareness

Involve the children in a kite making activity. They can either decorate their class or the trees outside with the kites they have made. They can talk about festivals when kites fly in the sky.

MATERIAL REQUIRED

———◆———

Any coloured paper, strings and straws / twigs.

A Little Turtle

Say the poem aloud with actions

I am a little turtle
I crawl so slow,
I carry my house
Wherever I go.

When I get tired
I put in my head,
My legs and my tail
And I go to bed.

New words

carry   crawl   tired   turtle

Let's read

A baby crawls.
A turtle has a shell.

88

Reading is fun

▸ How does a turtle walk?
▸ What does the turtle carry on its back?
▸ Where does the turtle go when it is tired?

Let's talk

▸ What is the turtle's house called?
▸ What other reasons can you give for a turtle going into its house?

Say aloud

circle	fire	cat	kick	quack
purple	liar	cot	king	queen
turtle	tired	cup	kit	quick

Let's share

▸ Imagine you are a turtle. Crawl like a turtle.
▸ Now you are tired so get into your shell and go to sleep.
▸ Wake up and start to crawl again.
▸ Now hide in your shell because some naughty children are near you.

Colour both the turtles

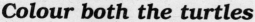

I crawl so slow   I put in my head

Let's read and write

A, B, C, D, E, F

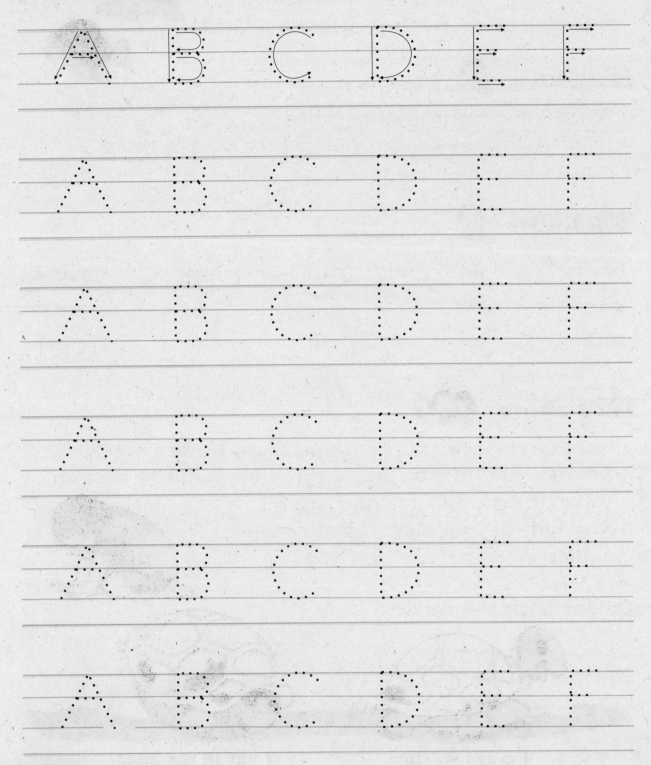

The Tiger and the Mosquito

Read and act out this story

A tiger was dozing under a tree. A mosquito came buzzing by. The tiger said, "Hey! Mosquito! Go away!"

The mosquito said, "Why should I go away? I am not afraid of you!"

The tiger was angry. He hit out with his paw.

The mosquito flew off. The paw struck his own cheek. The blow scraped his cheek. It began to bleed. The mosquito buzzed away.

The tiger struck with his other paw. The mosquito flew off. This time, too, he hit himself.

The tiger was helpless. The mosquito continued to buzz.

The tiger got up and quietly walked away.

The mosquito called out after him, "Don't be so proud, my friend. Everyone is great in his own way!"

Mrinalini Srivastava

New words

angry 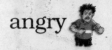   bleed   great   hit   proud

Let's read

I must not hit anyone.

I am proud to be an Indian.

Reading is fun

▸ What was the tiger doing when the mosquito came buzzing by?
▸ Why did the tiger's cheek start to bleed?
▸ Why did the tiger walk away?

Let's talk

▸ Why did the mosquito say, "I am not afraid of you!"?

Say aloud

bank	goose	fan	lamp
bin	gown	few	lick
biscuit	grey	field	lip
bun	gun	fish	loose

Let's share

▸ What do we learn from this story?
▸ Describe the lion and the tiger. How are they different from each other?

Let's write

Fill in the blanks by tracing the dotted words.

1. A _tiger_ was dozing under a tree.

2. A _mosquito_ came buzzing by.

3. The tiger hit out with his _paw_ .

4. The mosquito buzzed _away_ .

5. Everyone is _great_ in his own way!

Let's read and write

G H I J K L

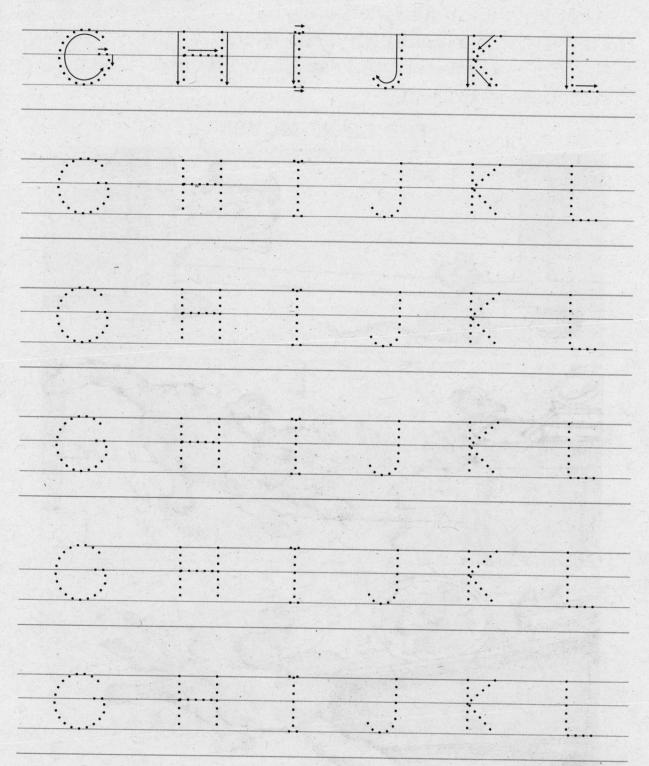

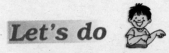
Look at the pictures below

▸ What are the cat and mouse saying?
▸ First say this in your own language.
▸ Now act out the story and say the words and sentences in English.

THE GIANT MOUSE

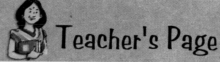
▶ **By this Unit children should be involved in**

- **Observation** of objects and things around them.
- **Conversation** about the observation they have had.
- **Sharing** of their own view point about the observation.
- **Reading** the text as much as they can, especially the new words. Encourage the children to say dialogues in their own words; then write the English words on the blackboard. Have a reading session of any story from the Unit. Let each child be given a few lines to read. Engage them in reading aloud with you.
- **Writing** simple words of one, two, three syllables (a syllable has one vowel sound, e.g. mug, truck, more (one syllable); never, lazy (two syllables) and September, October (three syllables).
- **Craft making skills** such as simple folding, sticking and decorating the classroom.

▶ *Use the method of developing skills in a very informal yet clear manner. The following should be kept in mind:*

- Development of listening skills — What the child **hears** is important.
- Development of visual skills — What the child **sees** is important.
- Development of sharing skills — What the child **feels** is important.
- Development of speaking skills — How the child is asked to **speak** is important.
- Development of reading skills — How the child is exposed to routine **reading** is important.
- Development of fine motor skills — Child's exposure to **pre-writing activities** is important.
- Development of writing skills — **This should be the last milestone in the chain**.

▶ *Raising awareness*

Encourage the children to brush their teeth after meals. As the facilitator you can add to this list. We must educate the children to preserve our natural resources at a very formative stage of their growth.

Clouds

Read and learn by heart

It is hot.
The sky is blue.
A little cloud comes looking for you.
More clouds come.
They bring rain.
Sing and dance.
It's cool again!

New words

bring   cloud   cool   dance   hot   rain

Let's read

It is a hot day.
It is raining today.

Reading is fun

▸ What is the colour of the sky?
▸ What do the clouds bring?

Let's talk

▸ What is the colour of the clouds that bring us rain?
▸ Do you like to sing and dance in the rain?
▸ What keeps you dry in the rain?

Let's share

▸ What do you like to do
  when it rains? (stay in/go out)
▸ Do you like puddles?
▸ The other seasons in India
  are hot and cold.
  Describe in your
  language which season
  you like the best.
  Now can you say this in English?

Trace along the dots.

Say aloud

cot	cry	drain	bring
dot	dry	grain	ring
hot	fly	pain	sing
pot	sky	rain	wing

Match the words with the pictures.

rain

children dancing

children singing

clouds

the sky

Let's read and write

M N O P Q R

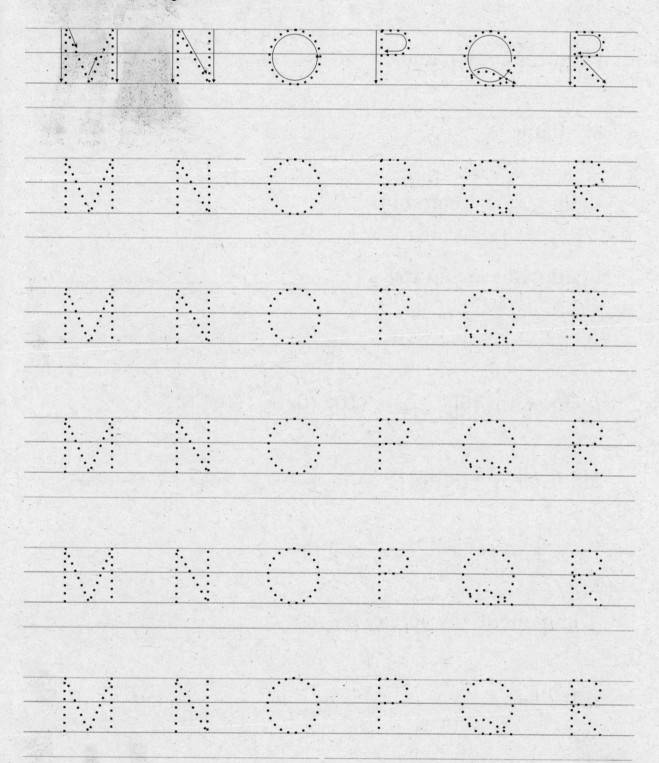

101

Fill in the blanks

I can read my name.

My name is _____ .

I am _____ years old.

I can write my address _____

_____

I can count till _____ . (10/20/30/40/50)

My teacher's name is _____ .

I study in class _____ (one).

The name of my school is _____ .

It is in _____ (city).

102

Anandi's Rainbow

Enjoy this nature story

It was raining outside. Anandi was fast asleep dreaming of rainbows. She woke up to look out of her window. There was a huge, bright rainbow across a clear blue sky.

Anandi ran out to the garden with Milli, her favourite cat.

Anandi loved to draw and paint. Today, she wanted to paint the flowers of her garden with the colours of the rainbow.

She coloured one flower with the violet, and another with the indigo of the rainbow. One with the blue and leaves with the green... One with the orange...

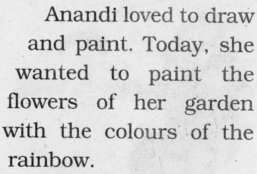

103

One with the red...

But she left the yellow so that the Sun may look bright and gay...

And lo! There were beautiful flowers all over the garden. The Sun was up there shining in its yellow glory.

After giving colours to the flowers and the Sun, the rainbow was gone...

Anup Ray

Let's read

A rainbow has seven colours.

Reading is fun

▸ What did Anandi see outside her window?
▸ Was she happy to see the rainbow?
▸ What are the colours of the rainbow?

Let's talk

▸ Have you ever seen a rainbow?
▸ When do you see a rainbow in the sky?

Let's share

▸ Go outside and look at the clouds.
▸ What shapes do you see in the clouds?
▸ Come inside and draw what you saw.
▸ Now describe your drawing to your friends in your own language and then in English.

Say aloud

face	back	lamp	hat
field	ball	leg	have
find	bat	let	her
fly	big	little	house
food	bought	log	hut

Let's do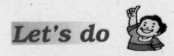

Look at the picture below. Circle the names of things that you can see in the picture.

umbrella

puddle

raindrops

house

cat

boat

mud

sun

roses

pot

mat

Join the dots from Aa to Zz and see what you can create.

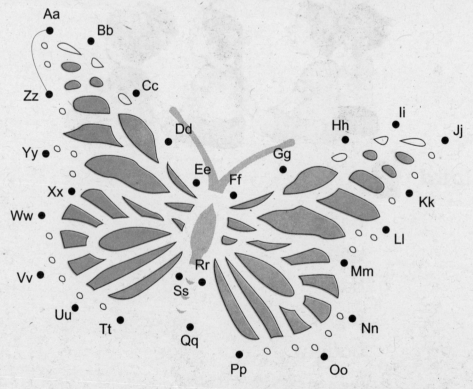

In the given space trace the rainbow and colour it.

Say aloud the names of the colours on the rainbow.

Let's write

S T U V

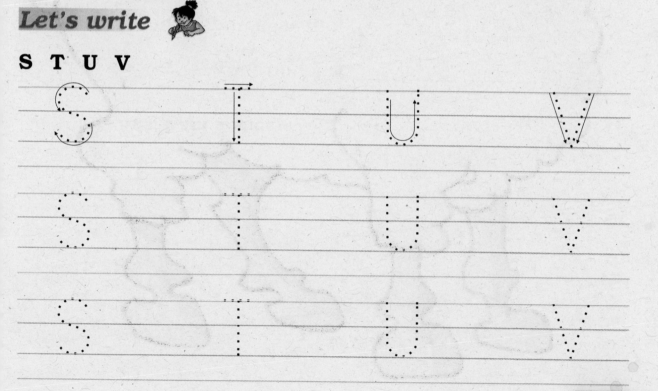

Let's make a riddle
Use _am_ or _have_ in the blanks.

I _____ white in colour.

I _____ two eyes.

I _____ four legs and a short tail.

I _____ wool on me.

What _____ I ?

Ans: I am a sheep.

The idea in this Unit is to assist the children in building their imagination; making and speaking simple sentences; and writing at least a few sentences. The sentences can be made both from the text and from their environment, using the sight words and flash cards in their classroom or outdoors.

▶ **Develop reading skills**

Let the children do the activity of **odd one out**. Encourage them to spot the one that is different. For example, draw a sequence of objects such as flowers and make one flower slightly different. Ask the children to point out the one that is different. These kinds of activities are relevant to reading as they help them identify and discriminate between objects and pictures.

Alphabet cards can be used for the matching exercise. The teacher makes cards from *a* to *z* in capitals and in lower case. The child has to match the capital letter with the corresponding one in lower case. For example, *A* with *a* and *B* with *b*.

▶ **Group activity**

Make a calender for every month showing birthdays of every child and display it along with this traditional song:

Thirty days hath September,
April, June, and November,
All the rest have thirty-one,
Excepting February alone.

▶ **Develop pronunciation**

Have a recitation or reading session of the poem 'Clouds'. Let each child be given a chance to read. The more confident he feels, the more motivated he will be to continue in his efforts.

Have a reading session of the story 'Anandi's Rainbow' from the Unit. Let each child be given a few lines to read.

▶ **Develop speaking skills**

Discuss with them the following questions

● How many days has September?
● Does February have 30 days in the month?
● How many months have thirty days?
● How many months have thirty-one days?
● When is your birthday?
● How many children in the class have a birthday in each month?

Ask the class to repeat sentences like: *'It's cold'*, *'It's raining today'*, *'It's hot'*, *'The wind is blowing'*, *'Leaves are falling'*.

Flying-Man

Read the poem aloud

"Flying-man, Flying-man,
Up in the sky,
Where are you going to,
Flying so high?"

"Over the mountains,
And over the sea!"
"Flying-man, Flying-man,
Can't you take me?"

New words

flying   high   man   mountains   sea   take

Let's read

The mountains are high.
The birds are flying in the sky.

Reading is fun

▶ Where does the Flying-man go?
▶ What does the child want to do?

Let's talk

▶ Can you guess who the Flying-man is?
   Choose your answer.
   ● The Flying-man is Superman.
   ● The Flying-man is a pilot.
   ● The Flying-man is an astronaut.
   ● The Flying-man is Batman.
▶ Now talk about him.

Let's share

▶ Have you seen an aeroplane?
▶ Let's pretend you are a pilot flying an aeroplane.
   (a) What will you see outside your aeroplane
       (i) during the day?
       (ii) at night?
   (b) What will you see inside your aeroplane?

Say aloud

mug	vase	wave	note
move	vale	wall	nip
mum	view	wax	knee
mother	van	wind	knit
mud	vote	why	knot

▶ Which word in the box sounds like 'high'?
▶ Which word rhymes with 'me'?

What shall I be when I grow up?
Match the following:

A person who sails a ship

A person who flies a spaceship

A person who draws or paints

A person who makes sick people well

A person who brings letters

A person who grows crops

A person who makes clothes

A person who works in school

A person who checks teeth

A person who flies an aeroplane

an artist

an astronaut

a sailor

a dentist

a doctor

a farmer

a pilot

a postman

a tailor

a teacher

Let's read and write

W X Y Z

W X Y Z

W X Y Z

W X Y Z

W X Y Z

W X Y Z

W X Y Z

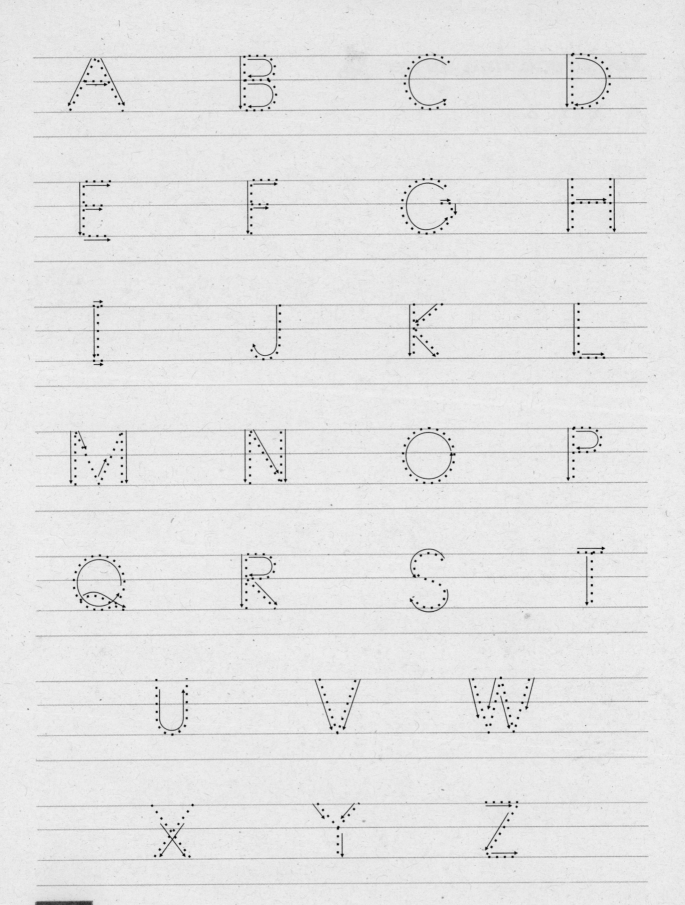

The Tailor and his Friend

Read and enjoy this story

Kalu the tailor had a shop near the river. He made colourful pants and shirts for children. Appu the elephant was his friend. Appu came to his shop everyday. Kalu gave him many nice things to eat.

One day Kalu wanted to play a trick. He did not give Appu anything to eat. He took out his needle instead and pricked Appu's trunk. Appu ran away in pain.

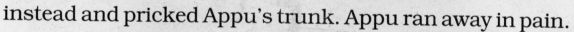

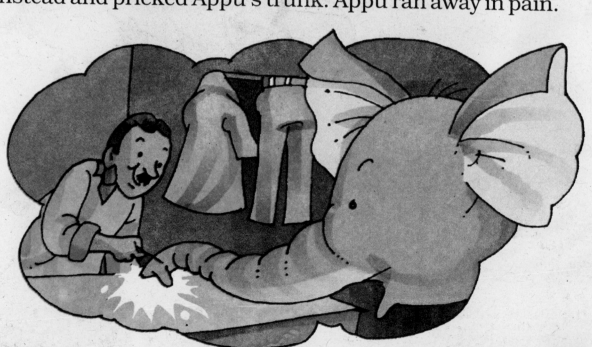

Two days later Appu came down to the river and filled his trunk with water. He reached Kalu's shop and threw water everywhere. All the new clothes became wet.

Appu shook his trunk and said "An elephant never forgets." Kalu said, "I am sorry, Appu. Let's be friends again."

Kalu and Appu became good friends.

New words

friend    pain   shop   tailor    trick   wet

Let's read

The tailor had a shop.
I have many friends.

Reading is fun

▶ Who was Kalu?
▶ Who was Appu?
▶ Where was Kalu's shop?
▶ What trick did Kalu play on Appu?
▶ How did Kalu's clothes become wet?

Let's talk

▶ What do you do
  • when someone troubles you?
  • when you are angry?
  • when you don't want to share?
  • when someone asks you for a pencil?

Let's share

▶ What games do you play with your friends?
▶ Can you walk and make sounds like an elephant?

The tailor had a shop near the river.

Question: Where is your house?

Answer   : My house is near _____

Make some more sentences like the above beginning with words like—

My school...   The elephant...

My friend's house...   The aeroplane...

The well...   My book...

Say aloud

jam	pan	year	zebra
jeep	pen	yell	zigzag
joy	pick	yellow	zip
jug	pink	yes	zoo
juice	put	young	zoom

Pick the odd one out. One has been done for you.

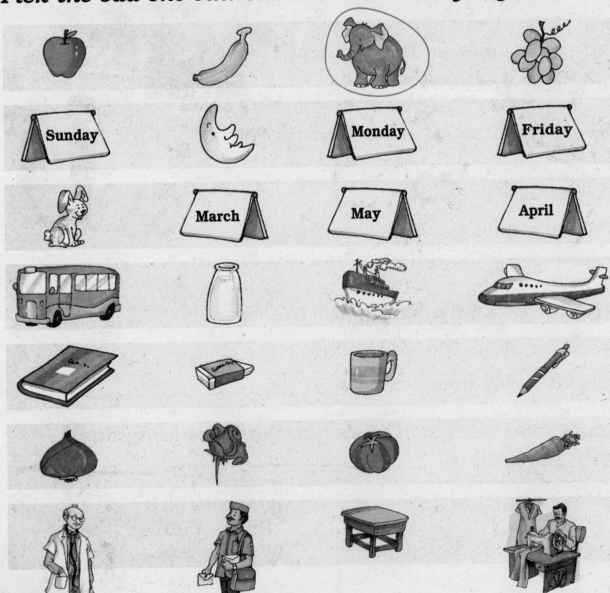

Let's do

Make a Friendship-band

▸ What you need:
  paper
  scissors
  glue
  ribbon

▸ Material to decorate (**sequins, beads, toffees, glitter, etc.**)

▸ Cut a strip of ribbon (colour of your choice). Cut its length to make a wrist band.

▸ Draw a marigold flower on the paper and cut it out.

▸ Decorate the marigold flower with glitter, sequins or whatever you like.

▸ Continue to make flowers until you have the number you wish to put on the ribbon.

▸ Glue the flowers to the ribbon strip.

▸ Let it lie flat until the glue is dry.

Now your Friendship-band
is ready to be tied
around your friend's wrist.

➢ You can use different materials to decorate each flower, e.g. buttons, lace, sequins, beads, glitter, toffees, etc.

➢ A wrist band with the name of your friend can also be made.

119

▸ The emphasis in this Unit is on:
- different occupations;
- imaginative thinking and
- the ability to write and speak sentences.

Children should be able to write sentences such as 'My name is…'

There can be times when the children do not speak correctly. Remember, the main focus is on communication and the ability of the children to express their feelings in English.

▸ Children can be given a series of oral directions to listen to and then follow. Gradually increase the number of directions. For example:

Pat your head,

touch your nose,

pull your ear,

stamp your feet.

▸ Encourage an **independent reading and writing habit** in children and provide them time for it. Motivate them by reading interesting stories and poems. Use the language for instruction that is familiar to the child. Let your enthusiasm for the story shine through. Speak slowly and clearly.

▸ Some thoughts on friendship, basic hygiene, and compassion for animals, peace and sensitivity to their environment can be discussed.

▸ Ask the children to practice the alphabets in lower case and capital letters. By now the child should have an understanding of basic punctuation like capital letters, full stops and question marks and be able to recognise plural and singular forms. In all this, the key word is **encouragement**. The child who senses your faith in his abilities will learn to trust himself and derive satisfaction from his accomplishments and stay motivated.

▸ **Role play and activities** are vital for the development of the child. Through these he/she learns to communicate verbally, share, take turns and enjoy interaction with others.

▸ This book attempts to involve the child in a sense of joy for a new language. The child who is gently nurtured, subtly led and exposed to all aspects of his environment is the child who will learn.

Enjoy this picture dictionary

Aa
apple

Gg
grapes

Bb
balloon

Hh
helicopter

Cc
cap

Ii
igloo

Dd
dog

Jj
jug

Ee
elephant

Kk
kite

Ff
fish

Ll
lamp

Mm
moon

Nn
nest

Oo
orange

Pp
peacock

Qq
quilt
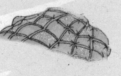

Rr
rose

Ss
sheep

Tt
tomato

Uu
umbrella

Vv
violin

Ww
whale

Xx
Xmas tree

Yy
yak

Zz
zebra